PRINCESS

DIANA

Royal Ambassador

by
Renora Licata

LAKE COUNTY PUBLIC LIBRARY

A BLACKBIRCH PRESS BOOK

WOODBRIDGE, CONNECTICUT

Published by Blackbirch Press, Inc.
One Bradley Road, Suite 205
Woodbridge, CT 06525

©1993 Blackbirch Press, Inc.
First Edition

Manufactured in the United States

10 9 8 7 6 5 4 3 2 1

Library of Congress Cataloging-in-Publication Data

Licata, Renora.
    Princess Diana: royal ambassador / by Renora Licata.—1st ed.
      p. cm. — (The Library of famous women)
    Includes bibliographical references and index.
    Summary: Examines the private life and public image of Diana
Spencer, who captured the attention of the world when she married Britain's
Prince Charles in 1981.
    ISBN 0-56711-013-4   ISBN 0-56711-051-7 (Trade)
    1. Diana, Princess of Wales, 1961–   —Juvenile literature. 2. Great
Britain—Princes and princesses—Biography—Juvenile literature. [1. Diana,
Princess of Wales, 1961– . 2. Princesses.] I. Title. II. Series.
DA591.A45L53 1993
941.085'092—dc20
[B]
                                 92-42255
                                 CIP
                                 AC

Contents

Introduction 5

Chapter One   The Girl Next Door 7

Chapter Two   Moving to Althorp 15

Chapter Three   A Royal Romance 21

Chapter Four   The Wedding of the Century 33

Chapter Five   Early Years as Princess Di 38

Chapter Six   A Modern Princess 52

Chapter Seven   Looking to the Future 57

Glossary—*Explaining New Words* 61

For Further Reading 62

Index 63

Introduction

Most of us can only imagine the wealth, luxury, and privilege of royalty. While many young boys and girls dream of such things, only a special few ever experience the life of a prince or princess. On July 29, 1981, Diana Spencer's childhood dream came true. On that special day, as millions around the world watched on television, Lady Diana married Charles, the Prince of Wales, who would one day become the king of England. From that day forward, she became known as Princess Diana or, affectionately, Princess Di.

A young woman, barely out of her teens, Diana began a new life as a princess. She was no longer a private citizen. And she no longer had the same freedom that she once enjoyed. Her life became both glamorous and demanding. To the best of her ability, she had to *be* good, *look* good, and

(Opposite page)
As a member of the royal family, Diana reawakened interest in the British monarchy.

5

do good at all times. Her days became filled with service, duty, customs and rules of behavior, and family.

Princess Diana accepted the challenges of royalty for the love of her prince and the love of her country. It wasn't long before she became one of the most famous, most photographed, and most talked about women in the world. As a "royal," Diana reawakened people's interest in the British monarchy (royalty). Such interest had not been seen for a long time.

As a princess in the House of Windsor (the name of England's royal family), Diana has grown gracefully into womanhood and motherhood. She has struggled to "be herself" and to have people accept her on her own terms. While conducting herself in a manner expected of a princess, she has also learned to express her own needs and desires. Princess Diana is a truly modern woman, one who continues to charm and fascinate the world. This is her story.

Chapter 1

The Girl Next Door

The Honorable Diana Frances Spencer was born on July 1, 1961, in Park House, in the same bedroom in which her mother had been born. Diana was the fourth child of Edward John Spencer, titled Viscount Althorp, and his wife, the Honorable Frances Ruth Burke Roche. Diana had two older sisters when she was born, Sarah, six, and Jane, four. Eighteen months before Diana was born, her mother had given birth to a baby boy. He lived only a few hours.

Although Diana's parents were thrilled that she was born healthy, they couldn't hide the fact that they had been hoping for another boy. In British families, when there is a title (name of rank or dignity) and property to be passed on, it is desirable to have a male child as heir. (An heir is someone who inherits the title and property.) When Frances gave birth to a son,

Diana, on her first birthday, at Park House in 1962.

Charles Edward, three years later, there was great joy, and Queen Elizabeth II was one of his godmothers.

A Storybook Home

Diana's father rented Park House, Diana's birthplace, from the queen. It was located on the edge of the queen's large Sandringham estate and overlooked about 20,000 acres of royal parkland. Park House was only a few hundred yards from the main house—the royal family's country home in Norfolk county. (Great Britain is divided into 32 counties.) When the royals would "go on holiday" (vacation) there, the Spencers were their neighbors.

Diana has always had a connection to royalty. She and Prince Charles have several royal ancestors in common, including King James I. (That makes them distant cousins!) Diana was born into the British aristocracy (upper class), but not into the royal family itself. Members of her family, however, have been both friends and employees of various royal families for generations.

Park House itself was a "storybook" kind of home. The house was large, but cozy and informal. It had beautiful gardens. Diana's father had a heated swimming

*

When the royals went on vacation in Norfolk county, the Spencers were their neighbors.

(Opposite page)
Diana at age two, on the grounds of her family estate in Norfolk.

✳
Diana's parents wanted their children to be raised "the old-fashioned way."

pool built for the children. The estate was a country paradise, complete with a variety of animals. The children had horses, rabbits, hamsters, gerbils, a dog, and a cat.

The Spencers employed a small staff to take care of the house, the grounds, and the family. Johnnie, as Diana's father was fondly called by his friends and family, and Frances wanted their children to be brought up "the old-fashioned way." Diana learned manners, values, discipline, and self-control at an early age. She was a lovable child, but one with a stubborn streak. Although she liked to please, she also wanted to have things her own way. Diana had a lot of friends and went to many parties. Sometimes there would be an invitation to the "big house," where she would have tea with Prince Andrew and Prince Edward. Diana was comfortable around members of the royal family. In later years, when asked if mixing with royalty made her nervous, she remarked, "No, of course not! Why should it?"

Diana's parents, Johnnie and Frances, were divorced in 1969. They both later remarried.

Diana's Parents Divorce

The peaceful, carefree days at Park House began to change for Diana in the summer of 1967. Her mother was no longer happy being married to Diana's father, and the couple agreed to separate. Diana's father decided that he would raise the children. With her mother gone, the adults in Diana's life tried to keep her busy. Diana was brave for a child of six, but she was often confused and sad. Sometimes she became very quiet and shy. Mostly, she tried to accept things as they were.

Like her sisters before her, Diana had begun her education at home. She had lessons in the nursery with a governess. Johnnie decided that it would be good for Diana to attend a day school near home. He enrolled her in Silfield. During her two years there, Diana's self-confidence grew. She liked being around children her own age. Her work was only average, but Diana always tried her best.

Diana, at age seven, poses with her brother, Charles Edward, in 1968.

Unfortunately, Diana's parents could not solve their problems. It had been a very difficult, unhappy separation, especially for Johnnie. He and Frances were finally divorced in April 1969. The court gave custody of the children to Johnnie.

Diana may have suffered more from her parents' divorce than most people realized. She appeared happy and carefree, but she often felt insecure and lonely.

Frances never stopped loving her children. She always talked openly to them

Diana, age nine, holds a mallet during a game of croquet in West Sussex.

about her feelings. Even after Frances married Peter Shand Kydd later that year, she stayed in contact with her children. Diana divided her free time between her parents. She was allowed to visit her mother and Peter on weekends or school holidays. In later years, Diana even vacationed with them in Scotland and has remained close to both of them.

Diana's horseback-riding accident during her early childhood also had a lasting effect on her. She fell off her pony and broke her arm. It took about three months to heal. She had no interest in riding afterward. This was considered unusual for a country girl of her social class.

Away from Home

At the age of nine, Diana began her classes in Riddlesworth Hall, a preparatory boarding school. It was a difficult adjustment for both Diana and her father. But Riddlesworth proved to be very helpful to Diana. It gave her a new sense of security. She overcame her initial shyness and got along well with everyone. Her spirit and energy returned. She was growing tall and strong and was good at many physical activities, especially swimming. Diana was particularly interested in the younger children at school and would lend a helping hand whenever she could.

Following a family tradition, Diana's father enrolled her in West Heath boarding school when she approached her teenage years. This magnificent country house, set on 32 acres of farm and woodland, was "home away from home" for the next four years.

The aim of West Heath was to "train the students to develop their own minds and tastes and realize their duties as citizens." Diana wasn't very interested in academics, and the school didn't push her in her studies. The administration was more concerned with fostering young Diana's good character and self-confidence.

Diana was very happy at West Heath, and she made some lasting friendships. She was allowed to devote much of her time to what she enjoyed most—dancing, tennis, swimming, and reading romance novels. She was a normal teenager who liked to have a good time. She played hard and got into her share of mischief, but she always kept her sense of humor. Although she didn't excel in the classroom, her commitment and kindness to others grew. These important qualities would serve her well as she developed into a young adult.

During her teenage years, Diana attended England's West Heath boarding school.

Chapter 2

Moving to Althorp

With the death of Johnnie's father, the seventh earl Spencer, in June 1975, life changed considerably for young Diana and her family. Johnnie inherited his father's title to become the eighth earl Spencer, and his children were also given official titles. His daughters became Lady Sarah, Lady Jane, and Lady Diana. His son, Charles, became the new Viscount Althorp. He was only 11 at the time.

Johnnie also inherited a magnificent country estate called Althorp in the county of Northamptonshire. The children were familiar with their grandfather's former home, but they did not want to live there. They loved Park House. Nevertheless, Johnnie moved his family to Althorp that summer.

Althorp was about a two-hour drive from London. It had been in the Spencer family

Diana always had a fondness for outdoor sports.

(Opposite page)
As Diana grew older, she developed a unique charm and a special grace.

The Althorp estate in Northamptonshire.

for over 450 years. The family house on the estate was enormous and very formal. The huge rooms had marble floors and were filled with fine antiques, priceless paintings, and rare books. Living at Althorp was an adjustment in life-style for the entire family. Diana often missed the more relaxed days at Park House, as well as her friends in Norfolk.

More Changes in the Family

In the months ahead, the Spencer children had another adjustment to make. Johnnie had fallen in love. The new woman in his life was Raine, Countess of Dartmouth. She was the daughter of the well-known romance novelist Barbara Cartland (one of Diana's favorite authors). Raine divorced her husband and married Johnnie in 1976. Diana and the other children were not told about the wedding in advance.

It was difficult for the children to accept Raine as the new Lady Spencer. For the past eight years, they had been the center of Johnnie's attention and affection.

Raine was a forceful woman who spoke her mind freely. She had her own ideas about things. There were numerous disagreements in the house, especially among Diana's sisters and their stepmother.

For the year and a half after her father's remarriage, Diana spent most of her time away at school. Shortly before she left West Heath, Diana's sister Sarah invited her home for a special weekend. It was a hunting holiday, and the guest of honor was Prince Charles. Sarah was dating him at the time. Diana knew Prince Charles, of course, but while she was growing up, she had been more in the company of the prince's younger brothers.

At this time, Diana was a pudgy teenager of 16. Prince Charles was a grown man of almost 29. He thought Diana was "jolly." Diana thought he was "pretty amazing." No one that weekend imagined that Prince Charles and Lady Diana would ever be anything more than family friends. Her schoolmates used to tease her that maybe someday she would marry Prince Andrew or Prince Edward. Diana must have chuckled to herself because she already had a "crush" on Prince Charles. She even kept a picture of Prince Charles in her room at school.

Out on Her Own

Diana returned to London and stayed with her mother in the city. While she looked for work, she took dancing lessons

✳️
Charles and Diana had known each other for years, but no one imagined they would ever be anything more than family friends.

Lord Spencer with his second wife, Raine, the Countess of Dartmouth.

Diana has had a lifelong fondness for children. Here, she poses with children from the Young England Kindergarten, where she was once an assistant teacher.

and attended cooking classes. Fortunately, she had money from her family to rely on. In the summer of 1979, Diana's parents bought her a flat (an English apartment) at 60 Coleherne Court. She moved in shortly after her eighteenth birthday. Later, she was joined by three other girls, Carolyn Pride, a schoolfriend; Anne Bolton; and Virginia Pitman. The four flatmates (roommates) got along very well. They shared the cooking, cleaning (Diana being the neatest), and expenses. It was a fun and carefree time for the girls.

Diana soon took a part-time job as an assistant teacher at the Young England Kindergarten in Pimlico. Most of the children were from upper-class British families. Diana was uncomfortable and shy with the parents and nannies (children's nurse-maids), but she was always wonderful with the children. Whatever she undertook with the children—dancing, singing, painting, block building, or even cleaning up— Diana did with kindness and love. She was doing the work she always wanted to do.

Diana's contact with the royal family increased while she was living on her own. She was very close to her sister Jane, who was married to the queen's assistant private secretary. Jane learned firsthand about the workings of the royal family. She would become a valuable source of support and understanding for Diana when she became engaged to Prince Charles.

Another connection with the royal family was Diana's maternal grandmother, Ruth, Lady Fermoy. Lady Fermoy had been in the personal service of the Queen Mother (Charles's maternal grandmother) for more than 25 years. The two grandmothers were dear friends. Some people believe they were partly responsible for bringing Charles and Diana together.

Some people believe the Queen Mother was partly responsible for bringing Charles and Diana together.

Chapter 3

A Royal Romance

Charles Philip Arthur George is the eldest son of Queen Elizabeth II and Prince Philip. In 1958, when Charles was 10 years old, his mother named him Prince of Wales. This is the honorary title given to the first male heir to the British throne. Charles has prepared since birth for the time he would become king. As king, he would be the symbolic head of Great Britain (England, Scotland, and Wales), Northern Ireland, and all of the Commonwealth. The Commonwealth of Nations is a group of many independent countries that were once colonized by Great Britain.

Because he grew up in a royal family, Charles was never allowed the freedom or independence of a private citizen. With the royal family's enormous wealth and extravagant life-style came responsibility, tradition, honor, and duty. Charles's life

(Opposite page)
Although it was not "love at first sight" for Charles and Diana, they quickly developed a strong friendship and a deep mutual respect.

would always be devoted to his country, as his mother's has been.

Charles was a serious, sensible person who thought things over before he acted. He knew, even as a young boy, what was expected of him. As the future king, he had to protect his public image. He served in the Royal Navy, commanding a mine-sweeper, and he also trained as an airplane pilot. As Prince of Wales, he often repre-sented the queen all over the world. As Duke of Cornwall, he also controlled extensive farmlands in the duchy of Corn-wall, a county in the southwest of England. He receives his income from this duchy.

Prince Charles was an active and daring sportsman, too. He enjoyed playing polo, hunting pheasant, fishing for salmon, and parachuting. In quieter moments, he enjoyed reading, writing, gardening, and listening to opera.

Because of his position, it was difficult for Charles to keep his private life separate from his public life. People wanted to know where he went, what he did, and whom he was with. While he was in his twenties, Charles dated many different and exciting women. His parents, as well as the British people, wondered if any serious thought was being given to marriage.

✳
With the royal family's enormous wealth and extravagant life-style came responsibility, tradition, honor, and duty.

Charles said in an interview once that he had decided 30 was "about the right age for a chap like me to get married."

But the prince continued to keep company with a variety of girls even after his thirtieth birthday. While he was enjoying himself, the pressure for him to marry was building. When would this "most eligible bachelor" decide to settle down? What kind of woman would be a suitable wife for the future king? Was time running out? When would Charles produce an heir to insure his succession to the throne? The press, the public, and his family were getting impatient.

Diana Is Noticed

Diana had several personal invitations to spend holidays with the royal family. These invitations did not necessarily come from Prince Charles. Although he was there on many of these special occasions, Charles was usually with his own friends. It wasn't exactly "love at first sight" for Charles and Diana. They didn't even share many of the same interests. After all, Charles was more than 12 years older than Diana. By the end of the summer of 1980, however, Charles had started to take a more personal interest in his new young friend.

From the time that Diana entered the public eye, she became a favorite subject for journalists and photographers around the world.

Diana had developed into a lovely, sensitive young woman. She could be shy and immature at times, but Charles was curious about her. He realized that Diana could be a trusted friend and a good listener. This was enough to begin a relationship. Once, when expressing his thoughts about choosing a wife, Charles had said, "Essentially

you must be good friends, and love, I am
sure, will grow out of that friendship."

Charles Courts Diana

Charles began to see Diana regularly. His
busy schedule did not allow him to spend a
great deal of time with her, but he enjoyed
her company whenever he could. No matter
where they went, no matter who was present,
Diana was herself—friendly and fun-loving.
She made no demands on Charles, which
was a "refreshing change" from some of
the other women he had known. Most
important, it was obvious to Charles that
Diana was very much in love with him.

By September 1980, the budding royal
romance was no longer a secret. One press
photographer discovered Diana watching
Charles fish on the banks of the River Dee
in Scotland. Determined to find out who
this new girl in Charles's life was, the
photographer worked fast. Soon Diana's
name and face appeared in major news-
papers everywhere.

No matter how hard she tried to carry on
her life as before, nothing would ever be
the same again. Everything that she did
became newsworthy. Charles was used to
crowds of pushy journalists who would stop
at nothing for a good story, but Diana was

not. It seemed her private life had been completely invaded almost overnight.

It was not long before 60 Coleherne Court became one of the most famous addresses in London. For five months, reporters and photographers practically camped out on Diana's doorstep day and night. She used her sense of fun to get

By September of 1980, Charles and Diana's romance was no longer a secret. In public, they would often be openly affectionate with each other.

through some of these tense times. Once in a while she even outwitted journalists who were following her by disguising herself or sneaking around them. She won the respect of the press with her good nature and determination. More important, she won the admiration of the royal family.

The Engagement

By 1981, Diana felt as if she were living in a fishbowl! All this attention was exciting, but sometimes tiring. In February, Diana decided to join her mother and stepfather in Australia for a well-deserved vacation. The night before she left, Prince Charles proposed to her in his apartment at Buckingham Palace. He thought she might like to think the matter over while she was away with her family. But she accepted his marriage proposal right then and there! In a later interview, Diana said, "It wasn't a difficult decision in the end. It was what I wanted—it's what I want." Diana felt, she told her friends, truly secure for the first time in her life.

On February 24, the engagement of Prince Charles and Lady Diana was announced. Diana proudly displayed the sapphire-and-diamond ring she chose for her engagement. This was a time for great celebration—in Buckingham Palace and on the streets. The long-awaited wedding of the future king was in sight. The British people had gotten to know Diana, and they welcomed her with open arms. The media had made the story of Charles and Diana into a "fairy-tale romance." If Charles had let Diana slip away, his future subjects would have been very disappointed.

Training to Be a Princess

Lady Diana started a very new way of life almost immediately after her engagement. She was no longer a private citizen, free to come and go as she pleased. A number of Scotland Yard detectives were assigned to act as her bodyguards wherever she went in public. Driving alone on the city streets, riding with Prince Charles to a social gathering, or shopping with her mother, Diana had to be protected—whether she liked it or not.

Diana soon moved out of her flat on Coleherne Court. She said good-bye to a free life-style and familiar surroundings. She was full of high hopes and excitement, but she was aware that the months ahead were not going to be easy. In a note she left for her flatmates, she wrote, "For God's sake ring me up—I'm going to need you."

The newly engaged Lady Diana now had much to learn. Being the wife of the Prince of Wales and the future king of England could be a most difficult job. (Charles often referred to it as a "job.") The first step was for Charles and Diana to get to know each

Soon after their formal engagement, Diana and Charles began to appear in public more frequently.

other better. Diana was given her own suite of rooms in Buckingham Palace, where she and Charles could spend time together, away from the public. Diana was not always comfortable in the palace. It was hard to think of this quiet, formal place as home after living on her own.

One of Charles's aides (assistants) felt that the most important thing he could do for Diana in the beginning was to try hard to calm her down. "She got very excited. She was always waving and smiling—like a film star. But there is a difference between being a film star and being a member of the royal family. Everything has to be more discreet."

As a royal, there was a proper way to do almost everything. There was a correct way to wave, a correct way to walk, and a correct way to shake hands ("always brief and never too firm"). It was even explained to Diana how she should treat the household servants. She should be polite when giving instructions, but never too familiar. This was certainly different from her relationship with the staff at Althorp!

Diana was almost a member of the royal family now. She felt the stress and loneliness of her new status. Charles was often

*

"She was always waving and smiling—like a film star," a royal assistant said. "But there is a difference between being a film star and being a member of the royal family. Everything has to be more discreet."

away on official business, and although there were plenty of others around, she depended on him for both support and encouragement. Publicly, Diana made an exceptional adjustment. In six months, "Shy Di" (as the press called her) began to grow into a more confident, poised, and mature young woman. She had a bold and independent style of her own, and the people adored her!

Dark Days

When Diana was alone, however, she was not the same person. She was unsure of herself. She found it difficult to be the center of so much attention day after day. The constant pressure that she felt began to overwhelm her and make her feel out of control. She became depressed and withdrawn. Some people who knew her during this period say that Diana even considered taking her own life at one point. The princess also developed an eating disorder. Not only did she lose a lot of weight, but she also felt weak and tired. This stressful and demanding period was the beginning of a long bout of self-destructive behavior that would endanger the health and well-being of the princess.

Chapter 4

The Wedding of the Century

"We still think about it; we still can't quite get over what happened that day. Neither of us will ever forget the atmosphere. It was electric. . . . It was something quite extraordinary. . . . It made us both extraordinarily proud to be British." This was Prince Charles's description of his wedding day. Diana felt the same wave of excitement but also added, "It was terrifying."

Breaking with tradition, Charles and Diana wanted to be married in St. Paul's Cathedral, London. Westminster Abbey had been the usual place for royal weddings. It took months of careful planning with attention paid to every possible detail to make things go smoothly that day. A total of 2,650 invitations were sent out by the royal household. Diana had been

(Opposite page)
In July 1981, the royal wedding was televised around the world. It was watched by more than 700 million people.

given 500 of these invitations to extend to her friends and family.

On the morning of July 29, 1981, Diana arrived at St. Paul's in a glass coach. The crowds looking on roared with delight. Dressed in a fairy-tale combination of diamonds, silk, pearls, and lace, this young girl was clearly no ordinary bride. Yet, like any other bride, Diana was nervous and excited as she walked down the aisle at her father's side.

The Archbishop of Canterbury officially pronounced Charles Philip Arthur George and Diana Frances husband and wife. At that historic moment, Diana became Her Royal Highness the Princess of Wales. As such, she was the wife of the heir to the throne of England, Scotland, Wales, and Northern Ireland, and future head of the Commonwealth. Their children would be princes or princesses of the realm (province or territory). As Charles's queen, Diana would become the richest woman in the kingdom. She would also be in charge of more houses, castles, and palaces than any woman in the world.

Millions Watched

Diana and Charles shared their wedding with a worldwide television audience of

more than 700 million people. As the
royal newlyweds left the cathedral, church
bells rang all over the city of London.
Huge crowds lined the streets, cheering
wildly, singing loudly, and snapping
pictures. Charles and Diana rode back
through the crowds to Buckingham Palace
in an open horse-drawn carriage, smiling
and waving as they passed.

The crowds followed them and filled the
palace grounds. During one of the palace
balcony appearances that day, Diana bent
her head so that Charles could kiss her. It
was the first time members of the royal
family had publicly kissed on the balcony
of Buckingham Palace. The crowds went
crazy! They continued to cheer even after

Diana and Charles returned to Buckingham Palace in an open horse-drawn carriage, riding past thousands of cheering well-wishers.

Charles and Diana went inside to greet their guests and enjoy their wedding "breakfast."

Peace and Quiet

After their exciting and exhausting wedding day, the royal couple prepared to leave for their honeymoon. The crowds followed Charles and Diana to the train station, waving and cheering. Always true to herself, spontaneous and friendly, Diana surprised those around her. Before getting on the train, she stopped to kiss and thank two people who had been responsible for organizing her memorable wedding day. Such behavior by a royal was unheard of. It was obvious to all that Diana was going to be her own kind of royal. Her natural, honest emotion was one of the things people admired about her.

The royal family portrait, taken on Charles and Diana's wedding day. Among those shown: the Queen Mother (in green, left); Queen Elizabeth (in blue, front); Prince Philip (back row, in uniform); Diana's mother, Frances Kydd (middle row, right, in blue); and Diana's father, Johnnie Spencer (brown suit in front).

Gifts Galore

Diana and Charles received more than 10,000 wedding presents from around the world. They ranged from priceless jewelry to farm animals! Queen Elizabeth presented her daughter-in-law with a diamond tiara. The gifts included nearly everything imaginable—carpets, lamps, paintings, furniture, and gold, as well as glassware, linens, silver, china, and much more.

The wedding of Charles and Diana was perhaps the most expensive in British history, but it also raised a great deal of money. For eight weeks, more than 1,000 presents and other articles from the wedding were put on display at St. James's Palace in London. More than 200,000 people filed in to see the exhibition and lingered at the main attraction—Diana's wedding gown. Profits from the admission fees and the sale of souvenirs were donated to charity. Many businesses benefited from the increased tourism that the royal wedding created.

Diana had made a fairy tale come true. Her youth and beauty helped to dust off the stuffy image of the monarchy. She was a curious mixture—regal, yet down to earth. When the people looked at her, they felt proud to be British.

Chapter 5

Early Years as Princess Di

 Prince Charles had promised the Welsh people that he would bring his new bride, and their new princess, to Wales. In October 1981, Diana, Princess of Wales, took her first official tour of duty through Wales. There was an overwhelming turnout everywhere Charles and Diana went on the three-day, 400-mile trip. Diana did not disappoint her fans, even though she was extremely nervous. On her "walkabouts," she moved freely into the crowds, shaking hands, talking with people, and gathering the flowers and gifts offered. Almost everyone welcomed Diana and was grateful for the chance to finally meet the princess. Even Charles was surprised at seeing his wife's popularity with the people. Charles once remarked to the crowd, "I'm sorry there's only one of her. I haven't got enough wives to go around."

Shortly after the royal tour of Wales, Charles and Diana announced that they were expecting their first child in June. They both were extremely pleased about the upcoming birth. Despite their happiness in those early days, Charles and Diana had personal problems.

It was especially difficult for Diana to adjust to her high-pressure life-style. She

A few months after their wedding, Prince Charles and his new bride toured Wales. Here, Diana enjoys her time in the spotlight, adored by the media and the people of Wales.

sometimes felt uncomfortable in her new roles as wife and princess. There was so much to learn about the royal way things were done. She was bound to make mistakes. Diana was hard on herself. She was afraid to disappoint her husband or his family. And because she was increasingly popular with the people, the press continued to cover her every move and pass judgment along the way. At first, the never-ending attention seemed like fun. Diana was flattered. But when she realized that she could almost never escape publicity, she became sorely frustrated by it.

To add to the strain, Diana had a difficult pregnancy. She suffered continuously from terrible morning sickness. Even so, she continued with most of her official duties. Royal responsibilities filled much of her day. With little time left over for old friends and familiar pastimes, Diana often felt trapped and lonely.

Motherhood

On June 21, 1982, Diana again made worldwide headlines. Ten days before her twenty-first birthday, she gave birth to a son. He was named William Arthur Philip Louis and would be known as Prince William. Mother and child were discharged

Ten days before her twenty-first birthday, Diana gave birth to the royal couple's first son, William.

from the hospital less than 24 hours after his birth. All was well in the royal family. Diana had given Charles a male heir. By royal tradition, Prince William would be his father's successor.

Diana had definite ideas about what it meant to be a mother. Both she and Charles took their parenting seriously. Although the British nobility and upper class usually place their children under the care of a nanny, the royal couple wanted to be involved in their son's up-bringing. They wanted William to be raised as normally as possible. Diana insisted that William's nanny be modern and informal, even though Charles would have preferred to have a more traditional caretaker. It was clear from the beginning that Diana was in charge of her son's care. Nannies were hired only to assist and advise the princess.

Worried About Diana

In the weeks ahead, Diana's health suffered as she became totally dedicated to her child. She lost a great deal of weight and seemed to have little interest in anything besides William. Charles and his mother were worried about her. Diana's single-minded attention to her son was partly a reaction to her new life as Prince Charles's wife. The Princess of Wales was not only depressed, but she was exhausted in mind and body as well.

Diana needed a break, but she hated to be away from William—even for a vacation. In March 1983, when it was time for her to join Charles on an official six-week tour of Australia and New Zealand, Diana asked to have her nine-month-old son go along. Understanding Diana's delicate state of mind, the queen agreed. Again, Diana broke a royal convention—such a young child of the royal family had never before traveled overseas.

The birth of their first child brought Charles and Diana closer together for a time. Charles seemed to enjoy fatherhood and came to more fully appreciate and admire his young wife. The prince and princess became national symbols of stability and family life.

The media kept constant watch on the couple. Charles and Diana appeared to be happy, but the unresolved problems of the past, and increased stress still tormented Diana. Charles did not seem able to understand what she was going through. Again, her eating habits became irregular and unhealthy, and again she became depressed and withdrawn. She often felt disconnected from family and friends.

The relationship between Diana and Charles was strained. In 1984, Diana became pregnant again. Charles did not hide the fact that he wanted a daughter. When their second son, Prince Harry, was born in September of that year, Charles was clearly disappointed. Diana was saddened by his reaction, and their marriage never seemed to fully recover.

*

After William was born, Diana became depressed and exhausted.

Diana and Charles's second son, Harry, was born in September 1984.

Royalty Never Looked So Good

Diana's tall, slim figure, fine facial features, and lovely complexion brought new life to the British fashion industry. She looked fabulous in all kinds of clothes. All the best designers were hoping to have the princess be seen in one of their creations. Copies of the clothes and jewelry Diana wore were being produced and sold around the world.

Princess Di became more glamorous and charming, and the public couldn't get enough of her. In the next couple of years (1984–1986), Diana developed into a world-famous "superstar." In America, as well as in Great Britain, major women's magazines reported record sales every time her face was on the cover. Her hair, her clothes, her travels, her marriage, her children—everything about Diana was popular. "She's the one we all want to look like," a 1984 Miss World contestant said. "The Princess of Wales is number one."

Diana's striking good looks made her an instant sensation with the British fashion industry.

Now that she was admired around the world, the challenge facing Diana was how to be happy. She performed her endless official duties and made her required appearances. And she remained devoted to her sons. But she and her older husband had little in common. Still in her early twenties, Diana wanted to do more of the things that others her age enjoyed. She wanted to break away from some of the protocol and restrictions of being the Princess of Wales. She wanted to have fun and wished Charles to be a part of it. Perhaps she felt that she was wasting her youth.

Unfortunately, Charles didn't always seem able to care about Diana's feelings or to understand her needs. Charles remained

Diana shares a happy moment with rock superstar Michael Jackson at a charity benefit.

preoccupied with his own interests and responsibilities. He usually preferred the company of others his age or older. So Diana stepped out on her own. As always, the press followed her every move. Charles found some reports of his wife's behavior embarrassing. He may not, for example, have appreciated hearing the Princess of Wales referred to as "Disco Di."

The Duchess of York

Sarah Ferguson (Fergie) and Diana had been friends long before they became sisters-in-law. Diana was thrilled when Fergie married Prince Andrew, the queen's middle son, in July 1986. Diana now had an ally in the exclusive royal circle.

Because Diana and Fergie had much in common, they trusted each other. They had similar childhood experiences (both had parents that divorced), they were close in age, and they had both grown up in the company of royalty. Now, like Diana, Fergie took on a royal title—the Duchess of York—and official responsibilities by marrying a prince. But it was the fact that Fergie was different from her that attracted Diana to her sister-in-law.

At 26, the Duchess of York was older when she married into the royal family. She had had more life experience. Fergie was lively, witty, bold, and fearless. She knew what she wanted and how to get it. Her father called her "streetwise," but she had an informal manner about her that put people at ease.

Diana admired Fergie's spirit and self-confidence. Diana was more sheltered and self-conscious after being in the royal "fish-bowl" for more than five years. With Fergie around, she could relax and be herself.

In many ways, Fergie was a country girl. She loved horses, and she rode well. This impressed the queen. Her mother-in-law

Diana and Sarah Ferguson became close friends when "Fergie" married Prince Andrew in 1986.

was an expert rider and eager to spend time with those who shared her interest in horses and the outdoors. The young duchess was also a great swimmer and a daring skier. To have more in common with her husband, she even learned to fly a helicopter! Fergie made an easy adjustment as a member of the royal family.

Diana and Fergie understood each other's lives in the royal family as no outsider possibly could. They were good for each other. They helped each other get through rough and stressful times with a sense of humor. They also shared the spotlight of media attention.

Diana began to spend more of her free time with Fergie and her friends, with or without Charles. She did more of the things that she enjoyed—dancing to rock music, playing tennis, dining out, shopping, sunbathing, and entertaining her friends at the royal palace. Despite her sometimes unconventional behavior, Diana entered into an important period of self-discovery and self-improvement. She would emerge in the next few years more self-confident and independent. She was getting older and getting wiser. But it did start people talking! "I feel sorry for the princess," one of her girlfriends remarked. "She can't do anything without running into a mountain of criticism."

The Queen Steps In

The press—and therefore the public— also began to notice that Charles and Diana were making fewer and fewer appearances together. In truth, each of them had a demanding schedule. In 1987, for example, the princess alone carried out approximately 175 official engage- ments—not including her overseas tours. It was not at all unusual for the Prince and Princess of Wales to attend different public engagements.

But rumors started to fly later that year. The press had found out that Charles had spent 38 days at Balmoral Castle in Scot- land, away from his wife and family. The press and the public wanted to know if the royal marriage was in trouble.

The queen tries to stay out of the private lives of her children whenever possible, but she could not ignore this situation. After all, Charles was the next in line for the throne. She made it clear to her son and his wife that they were following a dangerous course. The queen strongly advised them to spend more time together in the future.

Carrying On

There was truth to the rumors. The relationship between Charles and Diana was strained. The differences between them often led them in opposite directions. It was a confusing time for Diana. The young, restless, unhappy princess was faced with some difficult decisions. She had to consider what the future would be like with a husband who was becoming more withdrawn and distant. The constant media attention and the pressure from the royal family made her situation even more difficult.

In 1987, Diana visited Islamabad, the capital city of Pakistan, and spoke with youngsters there.

Diana visited with some children during an official stop in Nigeria.

In 1987, Diana and Charles must have felt that they had too much at stake to seriously consider a divorce. They couldn't risk disillusioning their subjects, the British people, or damaging the image of the monarchy itself. And, more important, they both wanted their children to grow up feeling secure and loved.

Diana and Charles worked out some sort of arrangement. They resumed their official duties as a couple at home and abroad. And they functioned as a family when it was expected of them. In the eyes of the world at least, the Prince and Princess of Wales were still together.

Chapter 6

A Modern Princess

In days of old, royalty was more or less self-indulgent. Except for the king and queen, the royal family did as it pleased, usually without public knowledge or criticism. Today, however, the royal family has work to do. It is watched closely and expected to actively serve its nation.

Diana has taken her job seriously and is devoted to carrying out her duties as Princess of Wales. It is a job that begins early each day and requires careful planning. When time permits, Diana likes to include regular exercise (swimming, walking, or jogging) in her daily routine. After struggling for many years with an eating disorder, she now tries to eat healthful foods. All these things improve her appearance and give her the energy to maintain her busy schedule. Diana explains a typical day by saying, "Imagine having to go to a wedding every day of your life—as a bride!"

By 1988, Diana was president or patron of at least 29 charities, and the list continues to grow. It is no wonder that her appointment book is filled every hour of every day for months in advance. Organization is vital even for social and family gatherings. Diana depends largely on her hardworking staff for the planning, scheduling, and arranging of her time.

Diana's top adviser and coordinator is her chief lady-in-waiting. This demanding position requires a good knowledge of royal protocol. The princess must be briefed prior to any public appearance. Also, any person or group expecting a visit from the princess must make the necessary accommodations.

When fulfilling her royal obligations, whether as a fund-raiser or a spokesperson, Diana is concerned with people first. She is especially committed to children's causes and the needs of the aged. She makes it her business to become familiar with the facts about particular diseases and social problems. Then she can relate to the people she visits and have something meaningful to say. (Diana even took the

As princess, Diana takes an active interest in the world's social problems. Here, she visits people at a home for the elderly in England.

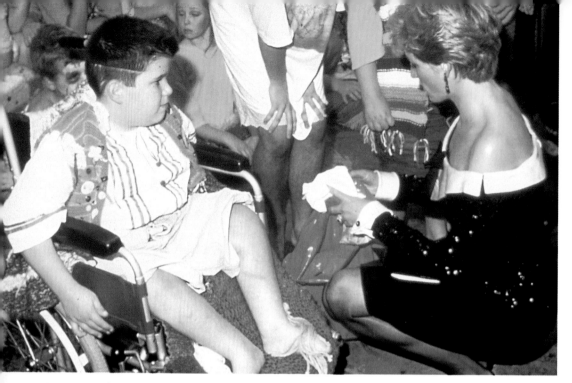

By 1988, Diana was president or patron of at least 29 charities. Here, she visits a facility for disabled children in England.

time to learn some sign language so that she could communicate with the deaf.) People of any age and in all kinds of sad circumstances seem truly comforted by Diana's presence. Her kind words, warm smile, and friendly manner make them forget their troubles for a time.

As patron of the National AIDS Trust, Diana believes in fighting the prejudice and ignorance associated with the disease. She made national headlines the first time she reached out her ungloved hand to shake the hand of an AIDS patient. Soon afterward, a journalist described that hand-shake as "the most important thing a royal's done in 200 years!"

In the summer of 1991, Diana rushed to the bedside of a friend as he lay dying of

AIDS in a London hospital. Her kindness and compassion were greatly appreciated by his family and served as another good example for the public.

Around the World

Both Charles and Diana travel extensively but not always together. Traditionally, British royal tours are meant to maintain goodwill with other countries and to promote the export of British products. Also, the many countries that make up the British Commonwealth of Nations (including Australia, New Zealand, Canada, and some nations in Africa) regard the queen as their symbolic head. As important members of the royal family, Charles and Diana are expected to visit Commonwealth

Diana speaks with an AIDS patient in a hospital. As patron of the National AIDS Trust, Diana is committed to fighting prejudice against people with the disease.

By 1991, Charles and Diana were seen in public together more frequently.

countries. Britain is also a member of the European Community, which means that Charles and Diana are likely to visit the major European cities for official functions. Traveling, with all its excitement, can also be hard work. On one exhausting 17-day trip, for example, Diana's official duties included 25 receptions, 7 lunches, 19 film premieres, 108 general visits, and the performance of 16 diplomatic duties!

In 1991, Charles and Diana were able to mix business with some pleasure. They took their sons (William, 9, and Harry, 7) with them on a trip to Canada. It marked the first time that all four family members had traveled abroad together. The trip combined several official visits with a much-needed family vacation.

Chapter 7

Looking to the Future

Unlike the president of a country, who is voted into office for a certain number of years, a king or a queen inherits a title for life. Throughout history, however, many monarchies around the world have been forced to give up their positions and their privileges. England's monarchy has withstood the test of time. The majority of the people still like the idea of a monarchy and are loyal to the royal family, the House of Windsor. Supporters of the monarchy take pride in royal traditions and state ceremonies. Although modern monarchs do not have the power to govern as they did long ago—today, in Great Britain, Parliament does that—they can still do important work for the country.

No Guarantee for Happiness

As in most families, the members of the royal family have their share of personal problems. Unlike most families, however, the price of being a member in this exclusive group is high. Each member gives up much of his or her individual freedom. The good of the family comes before the good of the individual. Duty and service usually come before personal needs. And because of the media, and public expectations, the royal family works under pressure. Life as a Windsor appears to be glamorous and exciting. But it is also difficult and stressful. The younger generation of royals seems to be feeling the stress, especially in their marriages.

For Diana, life as a royal is both stressful and, at times, lonely.

Fergie and Prince Andrew decided to separate after six years of marriage and two daughters (Princess Beatrice, 3, and Princess Eugenie, 2). This followed the 1989 breakup of Charles's sister, Princess Anne, and her husband, Mark Phillips. Soon after, they filed for a divorce. Some years earlier, in 1976, the queen's sister, Princess Margaret, divorced her husband, Lord Snowdon.

Throughout most of their marriage, the public followed the uncertain relationship of Charles and Diana. By 1992, the prince and the princess were living apart more than they were together. Many people were saddened by what seemed to be a total breakdown of their marriage. It came as no surprise, therefore, on December 9, 1992, when Prime Minister John Major addressed the House of Commons and announced that Charles and Diana were officially separating. Although the announcement stated that ". . . their royal highnesses have no plans to divorce, and their constitutional positions (future king and queen of England) are unaffected. . .," it nevertheless meant that the "fairy tale" had officially ended.

In March 1992, Diana was greatly saddened by the death of her father, Johnnie. Her loss only added to the emotional difficulty she was having as a princess.

Although her future is uncertain, Diana will always be thought of as one of England's most compassionate and beloved royal figures.

Third Lady in the Land

In 1992, Diana was officially ranked number three in the British social order (after the queen and Queen Mother), a most prominent place. According to long-time "royal watchers," no member of the royal family has ever been the center of more media attention than Diana. Diana admits that sometimes "being a princess isn't all it's cracked up to be." But as the Princess of Wales, Diana has performed beyond anyone's expectations. No one could have foreseen the impact she would make. She has touched the hearts and minds of people around the world.

What the future holds for Diana and Charles is unclear. Their separation raises many questions about their public and private lives. It is expected that Charles will one day be crowned king of England. But their official separation has caused people to wonder whether Diana would join Charles on the throne.

Whatever happens in the years to come, Diana has won a place in history. She became famous because of her marriage to the Prince of Wales, but she deserves to be remembered because of her own merit as a royal representative with a special kind of compassion and commitment.

Glossary

Explaining New Words

aide An assistant.

ambassador An official representative of a government.

ancestor A relative from long ago; one from whom a person descends.

aristocracy The upper class; nobility.

boarding school A school where students study and also live.

Commonwealth of Nations A group of independent countries that were once colonized by Great Britain.

custody Legal guardianship, or care, as of children.

duchy The territory of a duke or duchess.

flat A British term for an apartment.

governess A woman who takes care of other people's children.

Great Britain England, Scotland, and Wales.

heir The person who inherits a title or property or both.

monarchy A nation with a member of royalty as its head.

nanny A person who takes care of children; a nursemaid.

protocol The customs and regulations dealing with ceremonies and etiquette.

Scotland Yard The detective department of the London police.

subjects The people over whom a monarch reigns.

title A name that signifies an office or rank; a mark of nobility.

For Further Reading

Banks, David. *Sarah Ferguson: The Royal Redhead.* New York: Dillon Press, 1987.

James, Ian. *Inside Great Britain.* New York: Franklin Watts, 1988.

Levite, Christine and Moline, Julie. *Princesses.* New York: Franklin Watts, 1989.

Nugent, Jean. *Prince Charles: England's Future King.* Minneapolis: Dillon Press, 1982.

Rasof, Henry. *The Picture Life of Charles and Diana.* New York: Franklin Watts, 1988.

Turner, Dorothy. *Queen Elizabeth II.* New York: Bookwright Press, 1985.

Index

A

Althorp Estate, 15–16
Andrew, Prince, 10, 17, 46, 58
Archbishop of Canterbury, 34

B

Buckingham Palace, 27, 30, 35

C

Charles, Prince of Wales
    childhood, 21–22
    dating, 22–23
    early courtship with Diana, 21–25
    early meetings with Diana, 17
    engagement to Diana, 27–31
    honeymoon, 36
    marriage to Diana, 5, 33–37
    separation from Diana, 59, 60
    wedding gifts, 37
Commonwealth of Nations, 21, 55

D

Diana, Princess of Wales
    charity work, 53–55
    childhood, 7–13
    depression and unhappiness, 31,
        42–43
    early courtship with Charles, 21–25
    early meetings with Charles, 17
    eating disorder, 31, 43, 52
    engagement to Charles, 27–31
    flatmates, 18, 28
    friendship with Sarah Ferguson, 46–48
    honeymoon, 36
    marriage to Charles, 5, 33–37
    official duties and visits, 50-51, 53–56
    pregnancies, 39–40, 43
    schooling, 11, 12–13, 17
    separation from Charles, 59, 60
    as teacher, 18–19
    titled "Lady," 15
    training to be a princess, 28–31
    wedding gifts, 37

E

Edward, Prince, 10, 17
Elizabeth II, (queen of England, mother-
    in-law), 9, 21, 36, 37, 47–48,
        49

F

Ferguson, Sarah ("Fergie," sister-in-law),
    46–48, 58
Fermoy, Lady (grandmother), 19

H

Harry, Prince, 43, 44, 56
House of Windsor, 6, 57

K

Kydd, Peter Shand (stepfather), 12

M
Major, John, 59

P
Park House, 7–10, 15–16
Philip, Prince (father-in-law), 21, 36

Q
Queen Mother, 19, 36

S
St. Paul's Cathedral, 33–34
Spencer, Charles Edward (brother), 9,
  11, 15
Spencer, Edward John ("Johnnie,"
    father)
  death of, 59

divorce from Frances, 10–11
first marriage, 7, 10
at royal wedding, 36
second marriage, 16–17
titled "Earl," 15
Spencer, Frances Ruth Burke Roche
  (mother), 7
Spencer, Jane (sister), 7, 19
Spencer, Raine (stepmother), 16–17
Spencer, Sarah (sister), 7, 17

W
William, Prince, 40–42, 56

Y
Young England Kindergarten, 18–19

Photo Credits:

Cover: ©Jayne Fincher/Gamma-Liaison; pp.4,5: ©Georges de Keerle/Gamma-Liaison; p.7: Alpha/Globe Photos; p.8: Alpha/Globe Photos; p.10: ©Ian Swift/LNS/Camera Press London; p.11: Alpha/Globe Photos; p.12: Globe Photos; p.13: Alpha/Globe Photos; p.14: ©Kip Rand/Gamma-Liaison; p. 15: Alpha/Globe Photos; p. 16: Alpha/Globe Photos; p.17: Alpha Globe Photos; p.18 ©Tim Graham/Sygma; p.19: Bernier/de Keerle/Gamma-Liaison; p.20: ©Georges de Keerle/Gamma-Liaison; p.21: ©Hoffman-Spooner/Gamma-Liaison; p.24: ©Gamma-Liaison; p. 26: ©Georges de Keerle/Gamma-Liaison; p.29: ©Georges de Keerle/Gamma-Liaison; pp. 32,33: ©Gamma-Liaison; p. 35: ©Gamma-Liaison; p.36: ©Gamma-Liaison; p. 38: ©Georges de Keerle/Gamma-Liaison; p. 39: Photographers International/Gamma-Liaison; p. 41: Photographers International/Gamma-Liaison; p.44: Photographers International/Gamma-Liaison; p. 45: Photographers International/Gamma-Liaison; p.46: Photographers International/Gamma-Liaison; p. 47: ©Apesteguy-Georges de Keerle/Gamma-Liaison; p. 50: Jayne Fincher/Gamma-Liaison; p. 51: ©de Keerle-UK Press/Gamma-Liaison; p.52: ©Julian Parker-Spooner/Gamma-Liaison; p. 53: ©Parker-UK Press/Gamma-Liaison; p. 54: ©B. Shuel-Spooner/Gamma-Liaison; p. 55: ©Terry Fincher/Gamma-Liaison; p. ©Georges de Keerle/Gamma-Liaison; p. 57: ©Alain Morvan/Gamma-Liaison; p. 58: ©Julian Parker-UK Press/Gamma-Liaison; p. 59: ©Jayne Fincher/Gamma-Liaison; p. 60: ©Julian Parker/Gamma-Liaison.

Photo research by Grace How.